Martin Luther King, Jr.

A Buddy Book
by
Christy DeVillier

ABDO
Publishing Company

VISIT US AT

www.abdopublishing.com

Published by ABDO Publishing Company, 8000 West 78th Street, Edina, Minnesota 55439.
Copyright © 2001 by Abdo Consulting Group, Inc. International copyrights reserved in all
countries. No part of this book may be reproduced in any form without written permission
from the publisher.

Printed in the United States of America, North Mankato, Minnesota.
012001 032012

Edited by: Michael P. Goecke
Contributing Editor: Matt Ray
Image Research: Deborah Coldiron, Susan Will
Graphic Design: Jane Halbert
Cover Photograph: Archive Photos
Interior Photographs/Illustrations: pages 4, 7, 9, 13, 14, 18, 20, 21, 23 & 29: Archive Photos;
page 27: courtesy of Library of Congress, Washington, D.C.

Library of Congress Cataloging-in-Publication Data

Devillier, Christy, 1971-
    Martin Luther King, Jr. / Christy Devillier.
        p. cm. — (First biographies)
    Includes index.
    ISBN 1-57765-592-3
    1. King, Martin Luther, Jr., 1929-1968—Juvenile literature. 2. African
Americans—Biography—Juvenile literature. 3. Civil rights workers—United
States—Biography—Juvenile literature. 4. Baptists—United
States—Clergy—Biography—Juvenile literature. 5. African Americans—Civil
rights—History—20th century—Juvenile literature. [1. King, Martin Luther, Jr.,
1929-1968. 2. Civil rights workers. 3. Clergy. 4. Civil rights movements—History. 5.
Afro-Americans—Biography.] I. Title.

E185.97.K5 D48 2001
323'.092—dc21
[B]
                                                                    2001022019

Table Of Contents

Why Is He Famous?

Dr. Martin Luther King, Jr.

Dr. Martin Luther King, Jr. was a leader in the Civil Rights Movement. Dr. King fought for rights for African Americans. This was his dream. Dr. King used peaceful ways to fight for his dream.

People honored Dr. King with many awards. An award is like a prize. These are some of the awards Dr. King received:

- Nobel Peace Prize, 1964
- Man of the Year by Time magazine, 1963
- John F. Kennedy Award, 1964

James Earl Ray shot Dr. Martin Luther King, Jr. on April 4, 1968. Dr. King died fighting for his dream.

Martin's Family

Dr. Martin Luther King, Jr. was born on January 15, 1929. His home was in Atlanta, Georgia.

Martin's mother was Alberta King. She was a schoolteacher.

Martin's father was Michael Luther King. He was a Baptist preacher.

Martin's parents named him Michael Luther King. Later, they changed his name to Martin. His family called him "M.L."

Dr. King and family.

Martin had one older sister, Christine King Farris. He had one younger brother, Alfred Daniel Williams King.

On June 18, 1953, Martin married Coretta Scott. They had four children.

Growing Up

Dr. Martin Luther King, Jr. went to many schools. The first school Martin went to was Younge Street Elementary School. Then, he went to David T. Howard Elementary School. Later, Martin went to Booker T. Washington High School.

Many colleges honored Dr. King.

Young Martin was an excellent
student. His school let him skip 9th
and 11th grades. At 15, Martin went to
Morehouse College. College is where
many people go after high school.

The president of Morehouse College was Benjamin Mays. Benjamin noticed Martin. He thought Martin would be a good Baptist preacher.

Martin grew up as a Baptist. Both his father and his grandfather were Baptist preachers. They preached at the Ebenezer Baptist Church. Martin became a Baptist preacher at 17.

First Steps

Dr. Martin Luther King, Jr. believed in equal rights for all Americans. He often noticed unfairness against African Americans. Dr. King was African American. He knew that African Americans needed to be treated like all United States citizens.

In 1955, Dr. Martin Luther King, Jr. became president of the Montgomery Improvement Association. They wanted to fight segregation laws.

In Dr. King's day, there were many segregation laws. Segregation laws were common in the South. These laws separated African Americans from white people. Dr. King thought segregation was unfair.

Fighting Segregation

509
NO SMOKING
COLORED SEAT FROM REAR

COLLINS AVE.
TO HOLLYWOOD

In 1955, some city buses were segregated.

Montgomery, Alabama had many segregation laws. One law banned African Americans from sitting in the front of city buses. Only white citizens could sit in those seats.

Rosa Parks

Rosa Parks was one of the first people to fight segregation. She lived in Montgomery. She often rode the city bus. One day, a bus driver asked Rosa Parks to give her seat to a white person. Rosa Parks said no. So, the police arrested her.

Rosa Parks' courage led to the Montgomery city bus boycott. A boycott is when many people agree not to use something. A boycott sends a message. It tells people that you think something is wrong.

Dr. King and the Montgomery Improvement Association started this boycott. They stopped riding Montgomery's city buses. Other African Americans joined the boycott. This boycott lasted for about a year.

City buses are not segregated anymore.

In 1956, the United States said that Montgomery's bus law was wrong. So, the boycott worked. Dr. Martin Luther King, Jr. won!

Beliefs

Dr. Martin Luther King, Jr. tried to better the lives of African Americans through the church. In 1954, he became the preacher at Dexter Avenue Baptist Church. He was a preacher there for five years.

Dr. King preached about civil rights at church.

Dr. King was president of the SCLC.

Dr. King and other African American preachers started a new organization. This organization was the Southern Christian Leadership Conference (SCLC). Dr. King was president of the SCLC.

Mohandas K. Gandhi

In 1959, Dr. Martin Luther King, Jr. went to India. Dr. King admired Mohandas K. Gandhi. Gandhi strongly believed in peaceful resistance. Dr. King studied Gandhi's ways of peaceful resistance. He used Gandhi's peaceful ways to fight for civil rights.

I Have A Dream

Over time, people started to notice Dr. Martin Luther King, Jr. These people asked Dr. King to talk about civil rights.

Dr. King talking to reporters.

In 1957, Dr. King gave 208 speeches. People took note of his excellent speaking skills. Dr. King was good at getting others to listen to him. His speeches caused people to join the civil rights fight.

Dr. King had a gift for speech.

In 1957, 35,000 people gathered in Washington D.C. They cheered for equal rights for all. This is called the "Prayer Pilgrimage for Freedom."

Dr. King at the "Prayer Pilgrimage for Freedom."

Dr. Martin Luther King, Jr. gave a speech at this important event. He wanted the United States to give African Americans voting rights.

Dr. King is famous for his "I Have a Dream" speech. He gave this speech at the Lincoln Memorial on August 28, 1963. On this day, over 250,000 civil rights believers marched to Washington D.C. This is a very important moment in United States history.

Courage

In Dr. King's day, many people did not think African Americans were equal to white Americans. These people did not agree with Dr. King's civil rights beliefs. They made it hard for Dr. King to keep fighting for African Americans.

Some of these people took action against Dr. Martin Luther King, Jr. The police wrongfully arrested Dr. King several times. One person stabbed Dr. King with a knife.

Dr. King and his family were often in danger. Yet, he did not let these dangers stop him. Instead, he bravely stood his ground.

Dr. King was a brave man.

An American Hero

Dr. Martin Luther King, Jr. accomplished a lot in his life. He played an important part in:

- winning African American's right to vote
- desegregating Montgomery's city buses
- leading others to fight for civil rights
- improving the lives of African Americans

Dr. Martin Luther King, Jr. made the United States a better place for everyone to live. This is why he is a great American hero.

America celebrates this hero on Martin Luther King, Jr. Day.

Important Dates

January 15, 1929 Martin Luther King, Jr. is born.

June 18, 1953 Martin marries Coretta Scott.

October, 1954 Martin begins preaching at the Dexter Avenue Church in Montgomery, Alabama.

December 1, 1955 Rosa Parks fights segregation in Montgomery, Alabama. She does not give up her seat on a bus.

February, 1959 Dr. King visits Mohandas Gandhi in India.

August 28, 1963 Dr. King gives his "I Have a Dream" speech.

December 10, 1964 Dr. King wins the Nobel Peace Prize.

February 9, 1965 Dr. King meets with President Lyndon B. Johnson. They talk about voting rights for African Americans.

April 4, 1968 James Earl Ray shoots and kills Dr. King in Memphis, Tennessee.

January 20, 1986 Americans celebrate the first Martin Luther King, Jr. Day.

Important Words

citizen member of a city or country.

civil rights rights for all citizens.

Civil Rights Movement public fight for civil rights.

desegregate to stop segregation.

peaceful resistance fighting for your beliefs without hurting anyone.

preacher the leader of a church.

segregation laws that separate African Americans from white people.

Web Sites

Timeline of the American Civil Rights Movement
http://www.wmich.edu/politics/mlk/
This web page has won an award from the San Diego Union-Tribune's "Surfing the Net with Kids."

The Dr. King Timeline Page
http://www.pps.k12.or.us/district/depts/itss/buckman/timeline/kingframe.html
The students of Buckman Elementary School illustrated some of the major events in Dr. Martin Luther King, Jr.'s life.

Index